fast
fun &
easy

IRRESIST-A-BOWLS

5 Fresh New Projects, You
Can't Make Just One!

D1529962

Linda Johansen

C&T PUBLISHING

Text © 2005 Linda Johansen
Artwork © 2005 C&T Publishing
Publisher: Amy Marson
Editorial Director: Gailen Runge
Acquisitions Editor: Jan Grigsby
Editor: Liz Aneloski
Technical Editors: Carolyn Aune and Robin Gronning
Copyeditor/Proofreader: Wordfirm Inc.
Book Designer: Kristy K. Zacharias
Cover Designer: Kristen Yenche
Page Layout Artist: Kirstie L. McCormick
Composition Services: Happenstance Type-O-Rama
Illustrator: Shawn Garcia
Production Assistants: Shawn Garcia, Matt Allen
Photography: Luke Mulks and Diane Pedersen, unless other-
wise noted
Published by C&T Publishing, Inc., P.O. Box 1456, Lafayette,
CA 94549

Library of Congress Cataloging-in-Publication Data

Johansen, Linda,

Fast, fun & easy irresist-a-bowls : 5 fresh new projects, you
can't make just one! / Linda Johansen.

p. cm.

ISBN 1-57120-307-9

1. Machine sewing. 2. Bowls (Tableware) 3. Patchwork. I. Title.

TT715.J59523 2005

746–dc22

2004028554

Printed in China

10 9 8 7 6 5 4 3 2 1

Acknowledgments

Thanks to Jay Thatcher, always;

Evan Thatcher and Jay and Janelle Johansen, for
the joy and the friends you have brought me;

Merka Martin, for your warmth and wonder;

Alex, Kim, Libby, Marc, and Sidnee. I couldn't do
it without you;

Shady and Mocha, all day, every day, for as long
as we can;

quilt shop owners, staff, and teachers every-
where—they are our best friends, take care of
them well—especially my home folks at Quiltwork
Patches, A Common Thread, and BJ's Quilt Bas-
ket, you believed in me before I did;

Bowlers and Boxers, I can't thank you all enough
for your enthusiasm and kind words. I am hon-
ored to be part of your lives, and you are a very
special part of mine.

Thanks to the following companies for generous
donations of materials:

RJR Fabrics (fabric), Cotton Classics (fabric),
Timeless Treasures (fabrics), Timber Lane Press
(Timtex), C&T Publishing (fast2fuse), OESD
(Isacord Threads), Freudenberg-Pellon (Wonder
Under), and Olfa (rotary cutters).

Contents

Introduction

I started making fabric bowls for fun and to learn how to do something new. As I played with them and taught others how to make them, more possibilities kept popping into my head. The first fabric bowl book proposal I submitted to C&T Publishing included twelve bowls. Because there was only room for five bowls in the first book, *Fast, Fun & Easy Fabric Bowls*, we all knew there would have to be a second fabric bowls book. Here it is—and we've even included two more new bowls! Again, they are all reversible.

Through all three of the books, which included *Fast, Fun & Easy Fabric Boxes*, I have had the joy of working with a small group of dedicated fiber artists. You will see their bowls throughout the book. These women took the written directions for a basic bowl or box and experimented to see what would happen. How much could they change it before it became a whole different project? And then we'd be off on a bunch of new ideas.

I really encourage you to gather a group of friends around you who enjoy the same kind of quilting or fabric art that you do. You can challenge each other, and the brainstorming that can happen will elevate your work far beyond what you could imagine. One idea sparks another and they just build.

For the bowls included here, the ideas for variations just kept coming. The Pieced Bowl became a fun exercise in playing with geometry, as well as fabric choices. (I can't believe I said that! My high school math teacher would laugh with me now.) I had to make myself stop on the Double Square Bowl, so that I could get on with writing the book!

The Sunflower Bowl offered a bit of a challenge to make it fast, fun, and easy, but I'm sure you'll find the result is just that. Do you know how many flowers are out there that could become a Fantasy Flower Bowl? The pink dogwood outside my kitchen window inspired one, and as more flowers kept blooming in my garden, more ideas blossomed. Maybe the ideas wouldn't have come so fast if I were writing in the middle of winter!

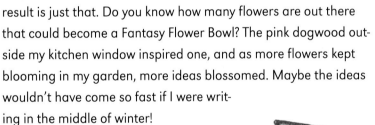

The Fluted Bowl is a definite favorite of mine. It's the one that graces the table in winter with a large candle and in summer with a beautiful vase of flowers.

I hope you will enjoy these bowls as much as I have. I can't wait to see your variations!

Keep on Bowlin'! ☺

Linda Johansen

Here's a handy guide for choosing fabrics and materials, tools, and techniques. Give it a quick read, then refer back here whenever you need some extra help.

Basic Materials

fabric

Choose a good-quality 100% cotton fabric that you just love. Your project will last longer, and it will be fun to sew. Once you are familiar with the techniques, be brave and play with other fabric choices.

Different fabric and thread combinations can totally change the mood of your bowl.

threads

I recommend using either cotton or polyester thread. The needle and tension disks can get warm with so much stitching, and some threads break more easily. Choose a good-quality cotton or polyester thread. I use Isacord or Mettler Polysheen for their strength and sheen. For satin stitch, decorative, or free-motion stitching with any type of thread, be sure to loosen your top tension to about 2.5 and use a top-stitch needle.

Cotton and polyester threads are a good choice to start with.

If you are having trouble with your threads, follow these steps:

☐ Rethread the top thread, then the bobbin thread.

☐ Be sure the bobbin is in all the way. If your bobbin has a finger with a hole in the end, try threading through the hole.

☐ Change the needle—be sure it's a topstitch needle.

☐ Lower the tension on the top thread.

If the thread still isn't doing what you want, change the thread. Don't spend your time fighting it. Use the same thread in the top and bobbin. That way, you won't have to be quite as precise with your tension.

interfacings

The projects need something sturdy inside the fabric layers to be able to hold their shape. They call for one of two types of interfacing: canvas or stiff interfacing.

fun!

Just because the project calls for one type of interfacing, don't limit yourself. Try it with the other kind and see what happens!

canvas

I like to use a 10-oz. cotton duck for my canvas interfacing. Two layers of it give me a sturdy surface to work with and plenty of stiffness to hold the shape. Denim and other canvas will work as well. Do not prewash. If the fabric has been washed, you might want to apply a bit of starch to the side you are not fusing onto. If it is washed, it will just be a bit softer bowl—no wrong answers!

stiff interfacing

You can experiment with different options to find the look and feel you want for your bowls. The idea is that you want the material to be light, to hold its shape, to be able to take the heat of an iron, and to be washable. The instructions in this book are designed to be used with 22″-wide interfacing.

One option is Timtex, a stiff interfacing developed for making baseball-cap bills.

Another option is fast2fuse Interfacing, a double-sided, fusible, stiff interfacing. It has the stiff, light, and washable qualities of Timtex but is already prepared with fusible web on both sides. This is a terrific product that saves time in handling the fusible. When using fast2fuse (available in regular and heavyweight), don't purchase the additional fusible web.

Both are washable and can be steamed to shape. Purchase either one by the yard at your favorite quilt store. If you have difficulty finding it, see Resources on page 48.

Your bowl will need some type of interfacing.

fusible web

Fast2fuse already has the fusible web on it. If using canvas or Timtex, you will want to use Pellon Wonder Under. You can use any fusible that holds the layers together permanently and easily; however, heavyweight fusibles may be difficult to sew and may gum up the needle.

cording

For a nice finished look I use some sort of cording or string around the edge of the bowls. It allows the thread to cover the edge more easily. I find it takes less time and thread. Use a 1/16″ polyester cording (made for clothing and pillow piping), a lightweight cotton knitting yarn, a heavyweight crochet thread such as Coats & Clark's Speed Cro-Sheen, household string, or whatever you find that works for you. You want the cording to be about the same thickness as your bowl sandwich when you are ready to finish the edge. Avoid lots of fuzzy fibers—that's what you're trying to cover! The color of the cording doesn't matter, but the satin stitching may cover more easily if the cording has similar darkness or lightness to the satin-stitching thread. (See Basic Techniques, page 9, for how to apply the cording.)

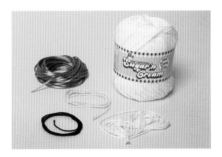

Cording will make those edges nice and smooth and strong.

fabric markers

To mark your sandwich, use a standard pencil or pen, or whatever is handy. When the marking might show through a light-colored piece of fabric, use a marker that won't show through.

When your bowl is all finished, and there are still a few spots that the thread didn't cover, get out the colored permanent markers: Fabrico, Sharpies, or other brands that work and don't damage your fabric or thread.

Be sure to sign your creation. Use a wide- or fine-point pen for your name and the date.

Basic Supplies

sewing machine

A good, basic sewing machine that can make a straight stitch and a zigzag stitch and that uses a darning foot is all you need to do any of the projects in the book.

sewing machine needles

You will want a sharp needle for sewing through the layers of fabrics, fusible web, and stiff interfacing. Size 80/12 or 90/14 top-stitch needles work best for me and make the project go much easier. They have a wider hole and deeper slot up the back to protect the thread as it goes through the fabrics. Choose the larger size for heavier layers.

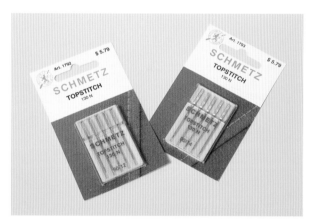

Top-stitch needles are easier on your thread and sharp enough for the job.

sewing machine feet

You will want an open-toed embroidery foot and a darning foot. I use an open-toed foot for all the surface stitching and the satin stitching. It has space on the underside of the foot to allow for bulky stitching, and I can always see what the needle and thread are doing. The darning foot is used for decorative or free-motion stitching as directed in the projects.

stiletto

A good stiletto can make a world of difference.

scissors

Whichever scissors you use, make sure they are sharp. I find my double-curved, duck-billed embroidery scissors essential for bowl making. They allow me to very closely trim threads and fabric next to the stiff interfacing, with ergonomic comfort.

A 6″–7″ pair of sharp fabric shears are good for cutting darts or stray pieces of fabric.

rotary cutting and marking equipment

A circle cutter works well for the centers of the bowls. Just set the measurement for half the width you want the circle and cut fused fabric following the instructions that come with the tool.

Compass points are a sharp point and a leaded point that attach to a 1″ × 12½″ ruler. They allow you to draw any size circle up to 24″ diameter, or larger if you use a standard yardstick. (See page 10 for more on cutting circles.)

An equilateral 60° triangle with the points included (not nipped off as for piecing fabric) makes it easy to cut the pieces for the Pieced Bowl. I like the Clearview Triangle Ruler.

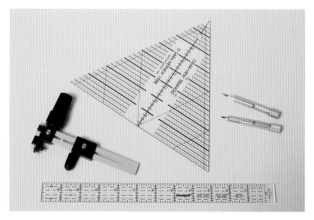

These tools make for easy marking and cutting.

easy!

ironing board protective sheets

Use a protective sheet under fast2fuse when you iron on the first side of fabric, and to keep your ironing board free of stray fusible web that might adhere to the outside of your bowl. Keep the protective sheet *under* the fabric and fusible. I like to use June Tailor or Clotilde Pressing Sheets, which are large rectangles that look like opaque plastic. I also use a piece of white muslin to cover my ironing board.

fast!

hot iron cleaner

Students tell me many tricks for getting fusible off the iron. Use a brown paper bag with salt on it and iron over that—it may work, but it's messy. Or use a dryer sheet and iron across it—they have too much smell, even without being hot! I recommend one of the tubes of hot iron cleaner and a thick padding of scrap canvas. Be sure to keep the iron up straight so that stray hot cleaner doesn't get on your hands.

Basic Techniques

cording

1. Set the zigzag stitch for a 1.5 length, and keep it wide enough to catch the edge of the bowl and cover the cording (approximately 4.0 width).

2. Lay the cording right next to the raw edge of the bowl. Hold the end of the cording behind the presser foot, and do a few zigzag stitches in place. Twist the cording as you sew to keep it tight.

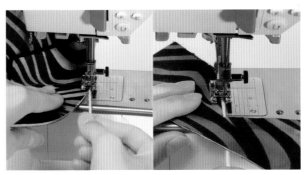

Cording around the edges uses less time and thread.

Move the cording to under the bowl on inside corners or curves.

3. Clip the cording very close to the beginning stitching.

4. Sew right up to the start of the cording, and finish with more stitching in place to hold the end.

Trim the beginning and end of the cording so that no lump forms when satin stitching.

5. Once the cording is attached, satin stitch over the cording all the way around the bowl or "petals." Be sure your stitch is wide enough to catch the bowl edge and cover the cording completely (approximately 4.0–4.5 width).

6. Set your sewing machine to a very fine (.5 stitch length) straight stitch, and take a few stitches along the inside edge of the satin stitching to anchor the stitches. Then trim the thread ends closely.

making circles

To make big circles, use one of the following methods:

Method 1: Use compass points and a 1″ × 12½″ rotary ruler. Set the pencil point for half the diameter of the circle you want (a 6″ setting makes a 12″ circle).

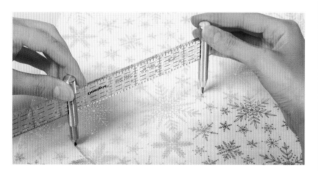
Use compass points to draw your circle, then cut it with scissors or a rotary cutter.

Method 2: Use a plate and a school compass to extend the circle. Set the compass for half the extra distance you want for the whole circle (a 10″ plate would need an additional 1″ on the compass to make a 12″ circle).

Extend the circle width using a school compass.

Method 3: Use a larger round template from around your home and trace around it.

To make small circles, do the following:

Use a circle cutter, circle templates, or set a school compass for half the diameter you need and draw the circle.

free-motion quilting

The Fantasy Flower Bowl (pages 36–44) is a good one to try some free-motion stitching on. The recommended stitching is just straight back and forth, and doesn't have to look neat and tidy.

Drop or cover your feed dogs. Set your stitch to a straight stitch—unless you want irregular side-to-side lines—and lower your top tension by a number or two. I set mine at 2. Be sure you have a top-stitch needle in and a darning foot on, then layer fabrics, similar to the bowl layers, for practice.

Sew while pulling the fabric toward yourself at a steady pace, then pull the fabric away from yourself. Try short and long lines to make a spiky circle. When you are comfortable with the motion, sew on your bowl.

easy!

Draw a circle on your practice fabric to help guide your stitching.

Practice the spiky free-motion quilting on layers similar to the bowl sandwich.

pieced bowl

This is a great way to use up your scraps of fabric and stiff interfacing. Or you may wish to simply take two fat quarters of fabric and play with some geometric shapes.

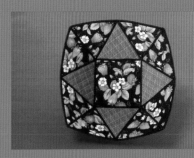

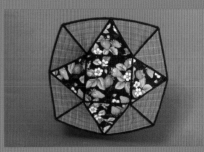

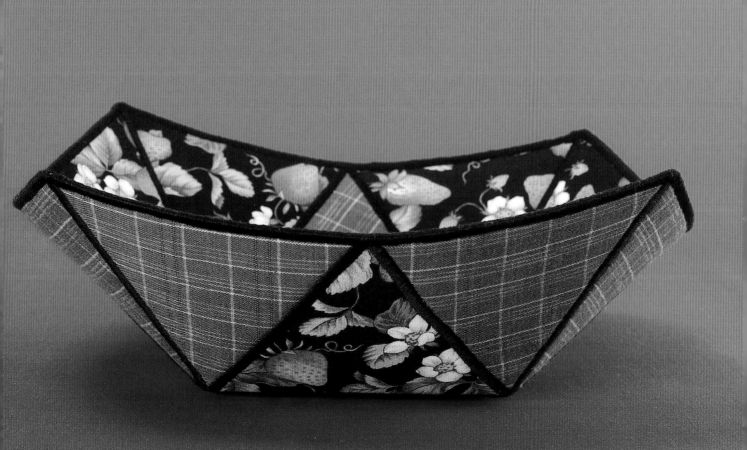

What You'll Need

- ☐ 2 fat quarters of fabric (or scraps)
- ☐ ½ yard of stiff interfacing (or scraps)
- ☐ 1 yard of fusible web (not needed if using fast2fuse)
- ☐ 1 yard of cording
- ☐ Thread to match or contrast with your fabric
- ☐ Equilateral 60° triangle ruler, regular rotary ruler with a marked 60° angle, or triangle template pattern on page 45
- ☐ Basic supplies (pages 8–9)

How-Tos

cutting

1. Cut 2 pieces of stiff interfacing: one 4½″ × 4½″ and one 11″ × 11″.

2. Cut 2 pieces each, 4½″ × 4½″ and 11″ × 11″, of fabric—one piece for each side.

3. Repeat Step 2 for fusible web, if needed.

fusing

1. Iron the fusible web to the wrong side of the fabrics first, then fuse one fabric to each side of the interfacing pieces. If using fast2fuse, just iron the fabric to each side of the fast2fuse.

fast!

I have not needed a protective sheet under the fast2fuse when fusing on the first fabric. A hot dry cotton setting on the iron works very well.

2. Trim the small piece to 4″ square.

3. For the triangles, cut the larger piece into 3½″ strips, and use a 60° triangle ruler or the triangle template to cut the strips into 12 triangles 3½″ high.

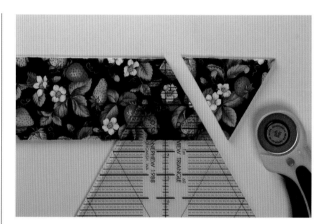

Cut the 3½″ strips into equilateral triangles.

fast!

Use up those scraps; fuse fabric to pieces of stiff interfacing slightly larger than the 3½″ triangle, then cut the triangles.

easy!

If you don't have a triangular ruler, use the 60° mark on your regular rotary ruler. Just lay the 60° mark of the ruler on the edge of the 3½″ strip and cut the angle for the triangle.

shaping

1. Sew 4 triangle pieces to the square base with a wide zigzag stitch (4.0 or wider). Butt the edges together and center the stitching to catch an equal amount of each edge.

2. Sew the remaining 8 triangles onto the first 4 with the same zigzag stitch. The piece is still flat at this point.

Sew first 4 triangles to the base.   Sew on remaining 8 triangles.

easy!

If your needle is punching the stiff interfacing or fabric threads through on the back side, change to a smaller needle. I sometimes use a 70/10 sharp.

3. Satin stitch over all of the zigzagged joinings.

fun!

Do all the satin stitching continuously by starting at a corner, going around the base first, and then up and down the side triangles.

4. Satin stitch the corners. Start in the existing satin stitching, backstitch a few stitches to hold the thread ends, and gradually pull the sides together as you sew up them. Pulling together too quickly will give you lumps at the start of the stitching.

Gently pull together sides as you sew.

easy!

You can zigzag the corners first if that is more comfortable for you.

5. Satin stitch over the seams again if you think the bowl needs it.

finishing

1. Trim the edges even, as needed.

2. Zigzag the cording on (see page 9), then satin stitch around the outer edge. Add a second layer of satin stitching if desired.

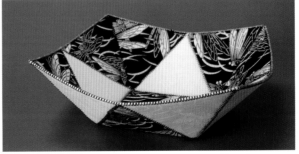

A black-and-white, zigzag-only pieced bowl

Variations

There are so many ways to use up scraps. Have fun with these variations and use the technique to make up some of your own.

A. Cut a small triangle and build a bowl of same-sized triangles around it.

B. Add some rounded edges to the small triangle base bowl, and you get a completely different look.

C. One large triangle base and decorative stitching, instead of satin stitching, can have a relaxing effect.

D. Use 4 small triangles instead of a large one and zigzag the triangles together for a bowl with stiffer edges and sharper corners.

E. Try it with a pentagon base. Just match the sides of the triangle to the length of the pentagon sides.

F. A pentagon base with hexagon sides easily becomes a soccer ball for the soccer mom or soccer player.

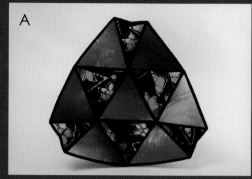

Small tri-base bowl, by Linda Johansen

Small tri-base bowl with rounded corners, by Alex Vincent

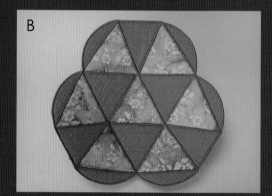

Large tri-base chameleon bowl, by Libby Ankarberg

Four small tri-base bowl, by Linda Johansen

Soccer bowl,
by Linda Johansen

Pent-base bowl, by Linda Johansen

Double Square Bowl

Double the pleasure and the fun, but still fast, fun, and easy! I found so many ways to vary the Double Square Bowl that I had to stop myself in order to finish the book. Take double the time, try half the size, or other sizes—and spend some time playing with this one.

What You'll Need

- [ ] 2 fat quarters of coordinating fabrics
- [ ] 2 scraps, approximately 4½″ square, and 2 scraps, approximately 6½″ square, of coordinating fabric for bases
- [ ] ½ yard of stiff interfacing
- [ ] 1½ yards of fusible web (⅓ yard if using fast2fuse)
- [ ] 1¾ yards of cording

- [ ] Thread to match or contrast with fabrics
- [ ] 18″ square of template material (optional)
- [ ] 12½″ square rotary ruler
- [ ] 20″ or longer ruler
- [ ] Basic supplies (pages 8–9)

How-Tos

making the pattern

1. Draw around a 12½″ square ruler on a piece of template material or stiff interfacing.

2. Draw lines through the diagonals, corner to corner.

3. Rotate the ruler 45° and center it on the diagonal lines you just drew, so that the 6¼″ marks on the ruler are on the diagonal lines.

Mark lines around the square and through the diagonals.

Mark the second square onto the pattern.

fun!

This bowl can be made larger or smaller quite easily with all the different sizes of square rulers on the market.

easy!

Make a plastic template, or save a piece of stiff interfacing marked this way to use as a template.

4. Cut out the template. Cut the inside corners carefully with scissors.

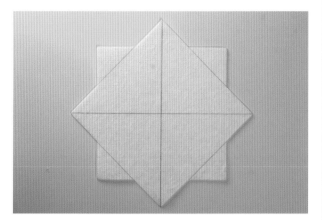

Finished interfacing template

layering

1. Stack the 2 fat quarters right sides together with 2 layers of fusible web, fusible sides together, on top. Omit the fusible web if using fast2fuse.

2. Lay the cut stiff interfacing piece on top, and cut all layers ½˝ larger all around.

Use the stiff interfacing pattern to cut the fabric ½˝ larger all around.

3. Make sure the fabric is smooth with no wrinkles, and iron the fusible web to the fabric. If you are using fast2fuse, iron the fabric to the fast2fuse.

4. Fuse a piece of fabric on the interfacing, and then trim it to the edge of the stiff interfacing.

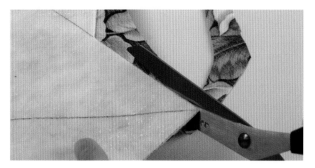

Trim the first fused fabric to the edge of the interfacing.

5. Fuse the second piece of fabric on the other side, and trim it to the edge of the sandwich.

fast!

Fuse fabric onto both sides of an uncut piece of stiff interfacing first, and use a template to cut out the sandwich.

adding the bases

1. Apply the fusible web to the two 4½˝ and two 6½˝ square pieces of base fabrics.

2. Trim them down to 4˝ and 5¾˝ squares.

3. Draw a dart line on the sandwich from one valley corner to the corner directly across from it. Draw only on the side of the bowl that will show the lines best.

4. Draw a second dart line perpendicular to the first, from valley corner to valley corner.

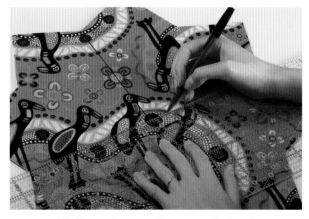

Mark two placement lines across the bowl.

5. Make a small mark at the center of each side of one 5¾˝ base fabric. Do this only on the piece that will go on the side of the bowl with the already marked dart lines.

6. Center this piece with each side center mark on a dart line.

Large base centered on the placement lines

7. Fuse on the large base.

8. Sew "in the ditch" around the edge of the base. This provides a guideline for placement of the large base on the other side.

Straight stitch "in the ditch" around the base.

9. Fuse the large base on the other side, centering it within the sewn lines.

Fuse the second large base inside the sewn guidelines.

10. Center one of the 4˝ bases, with its points on the center of the sides of the larger base, at the marked lines. Fuse it on.

Center the second base over the first.

11. Sew "in the ditch" around this smaller base. Turn the sandwich over and fuse the other small base inside the sewn lines.

Check out the variations on page 21, and play with the number of centers!

12. Set your machine to a satin stitch (4.0–4.5 width, .2 length), and test your stitches on a sandwiched scrap of the same layers you are sewing on.

13. Satin stitch around the edges of both bases.

easy!

Change thread colors on each of the bases for an added design element.

fun!

If you have used a larger base on only one side, the stitches will be entirely decorative on the other side.

Shaping

1. Make a mark ⅜″ to each side of the 4 dart lines already drawn.

2. Draw a line from each edge mark to meet the center line ¼″ out from the base.

3. Repeat this on each side of the dart line for all 4 darts.

Draw the dart lines.

easy!

If you are not certain how you want to dart it, practice with paper. Draw the outer edges, and try some different sizes or shapes of darts.

4. Cut out each dart.

Cut out a dart.

5. Be sure your machine is set for a satin stitch, 4.0–4.5 width and .2 length.

6. Place the narrow end of the dart under the machine. Begin by backstitching a few stitches, then gently and slowly pull the dart together as you satin stitch up the length. Center the stitching so it catches each side of the dart evenly.

Gently pull the dart together and center the stitching to evenly catch each side.

7. Sew each dart this way.

Finishing

1. Zigzag the cording on (page 9) and then satin stitch around the outer edge. Add a second layer of satin stitching if you think it needs it.

2. Be sure to sign your bowl!

fun!

Add decorative stitching to complement the lines added by the second center. Try some fancy stitches if your machine has them.

easy!

Round the corners very slightly to make the corners a bit easier to sew around. A small spool of thread makes a great "template" for this. You can cut them even more rounded for a very different-looking bowl.

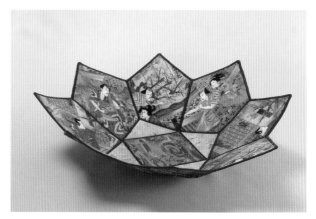

Another version of the Double Square Bowl

fast!

Zigzag some rayon rat-tail cording on instead of satin stitching.

Double your fun and the possibilities will just keep coming!

Variations

Once you get started on Double Square Bowls, you won't want to quit. There are just too many ways to make them.

A. This variation uses hand-dyed fabrics and only one center. Accent lines are made with strong contrast thread.

B. By cutting squares smaller and smaller in graduated hand-dyed fabrics, you can create a dinner plate dahlia.

C. Elongating four points makes for a unique twinkling star bowl.

D. Elongating all eight points turns it into a great spiky bowl.

E. The bowls can be made any size. This one used a 9" square pattern.

F. A set's a good bet. Each bowl started 2˝ smaller than the one it sits in, with a proportionally smaller base (12˝, 10˝, 8˝, 6˝, and 4˝). For each smaller size, shorten the darts a bit, and make them narrower by about ¹⁄₁₆˝ on each side.

Single center and accent stitching, by Linda Johansen

Green and yellow dinner place dahlia, by Linda Johansen

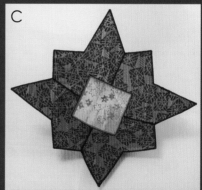

Twinkling star bowl, by Sidnee Snell

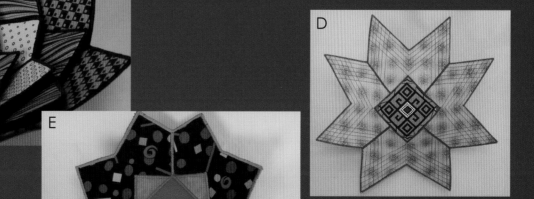

Great green spiky bowl, by Sidnee Snell

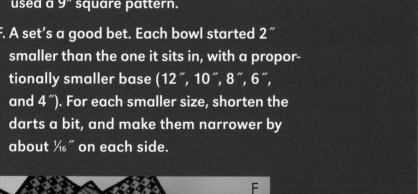

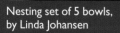

Nesting set of 5 bowls,
by Linda Johansen

Small bowl with two centers, by Marc Kemper

sunflower bowl

Spread some sunshine around your home with a few of these sunny faces.

What You'll Need

- ☐ 2 fat quarters of "sunny" fabrics
- ☐ 2 scraps, approximately 4″ square, of fabric for flower center
- ☐ ½ yard of canvas, denim, or duck fabric
- ☐ 1 yard of fusible web
- ☐ 1¼ yards of cording
- ☐ Thread to contrast with your flower fabric
- ☐ Temporary adhesive basting spray
- ☐ Freezer paper (6″ × 15″)
- ☐ Topstitch needle (90/16)
- ☐ Pattern for petals (page 45)
- ☐ Basic supplies (pages 8–9)

How-Tos

Layering

1. Apply fusible web to the wrong side of two 13″ squares of fabric. Peel the paper backing from the fabric squares, and fuse each of them to a 13″ square of canvas.

fun!

The "wrong" side of the fabric is your choice—you pay for both sides!

2. Draw a 12″ circle on each of the fused squares, and cut them out using scissors or a large rotary cutter. See page 10 for circle making methods.

easy!

Mark one circle, stack the layers, put a dinner plate upside down to firmly hold the sandwich, press firmly with a rotary cutter, and cut both pieces at the same time.

fast!

Be brave—stack the layers and freehand cut your circles.

3. Spray the canvas side of a circle with a temporary spray adhesive.

4. Layer the circles on a flat surface with canvas sides together, and press firmly with your hand. If the layers do not hold together, try spraying both sides *lightly*. Overspraying will gum up your needle when you sew the sides.

Adding the Bases

1. Apply fusible web to two 4″ scraps of canvas.

2. Apply fusible web to the back of 2 scraps of fabric, at least 4″ squares. They must be larger than the canvas scraps. These fabrics will be the center of your "flower" and the base of the bowl.

3. Freehand cut a circle about 3″–3½″ from one piece of canvas, or use a school compass or circle cutter to make your circle (page 10). Make this circle about ¼″ smaller around than you want the base.

4. Lay a piece of the base fabric over the cut canvas piece, and cut it ¹⁄₁₆″ larger all around than the canvas base. This piece should be the size you want your center. If you cut these freehand, place a pin in the same direction on each of them so that you can match the shape when they get fused.

Keep one fabric and one canvas scrap with fusible on the back, uncut.

5. Place the canvas circle in the center of the bowl sandwich—eyeball it; flowers aren't perfect! Fuse in place. Leave in the directional pin.

Match the direction of the pins on the cut canvas and fabric bases.

easy!

Use flat-headed flower pins to keep track of freehand-cut centers. Leave them in until you place the first fabric base over the canvas base.

6. Center the second, untrimmed canvas scrap on the other side of the fabric sandwich. Check to be sure that it is centered over the first base.

7. With the untrimmed scrap on the bottom, straight stitch around the cutout base. Sew about ¹⁄₁₆″ inside the edge.

Straight stitch ¹⁄₁₆″ inside the edge of the cut base.

8. Turn the sandwich over, and trim away the canvas that extends outside the stitching. Use your double-curved, duck-billed scissors, and pull up on the fabric as you are trimming. This will give you a nice close trim, and the edges of the bases will line up perfectly.

Pull up on the edge as you cut to a get a close trim.

9. Fuse the second canvas base in place.

10. Fuse the cut fabric base over the first canvas base, matching the directional pins or centering it.

Match the base pins before fusing.

11. Sew and trim the fabric bases the same way you did the canvas bases. Iron the fabrics to be sure the bases are well fused.

12. Stitch within the base to stabilize all the layers. A double-zigzag mending stitch works well for the base to make it really look like sunflower seeds. Begin stitching around the outer edge of the base, and sew more slowly and turn the sandwich faster as you get toward the center.

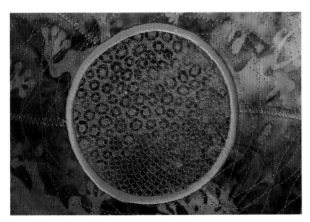

Sew some fun, easy stitches in the center, like this double-zigzag mending stitch.

fun!

Do your center stitching to look like stamens, bugs, or seeds on the flower!

13. Satin stitch around the edge of the base using a 4.0 stitch width. Center the stitch between the edge of the base and the stitching line just inside the edge so your stitches will be sure to cover the edge of the base on the reverse side.

Satin stitch around the edge of the base.

Quilting

1. Use a decorative thread, and sew around the bowl with a wavy spiral. Start to the right of the center, and sew with the sandwich moving counterclockwise. This keeps the bulk of the sandwich to the left of the sewing machine arm rather than under it.

Sew so that the sandwich moves counterclockwise.

> Play with the stitching. Draw your petals and darts before sewing the sides and embellish the petals differently than the background.

Shaping

1. Using the pattern on page 45, trace the petal, with the dart, onto freezer paper. Pin together 6 layers of freezer paper, and cut out 6 petals including the dart on each side. While the layers are still pinned together, mark the darts through all the layers by stitching along the petal dart lines with an old needle and no thread in your machine.

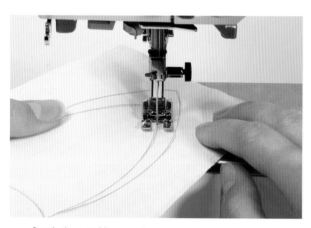

Stitch the petal lines with an old needle and no thread.

fast!

> After you trace the petal pattern on a piece of freezer paper, iron 7 layers together, with the drawn pattern on top. Lightly iron the layers onto the stack, one at a time. The layers won't shift while you cut them!

2. Arrange the freezer paper petals onto the sandwich. There should be about ¼˝ between the petals at the base of the bowl. Restack and pin the petals and trim slightly if necessary. The petal points may extend a bit beyond the edge of the sandwich. This is okay. Iron the petals on the sandwich.

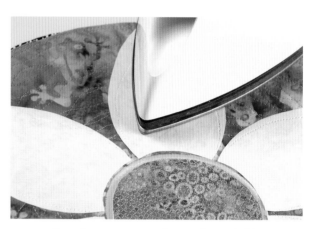

Press freezer paper petals onto the sandwich.

fast!

> Draw the petals and darts on the sandwich freehand.

3. Cut along the outside dart edges on each side of the petal. Then, cut straight in from the edge to the tip of the petal.

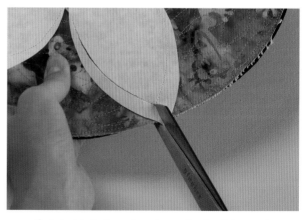

Cut straight in from the edge to the tip of the petal.

fun!

To make the petals extend beyond the bowl edge, begin cutting the petal at the edge of the bowl rather than cutting straight in first. Take the same darts from either side of the petal, cutting away some of the edge. When the darts are sewn, the sides won't come to the end of the petal.

4. Cut along the inside edge of the dart, and remove the dart. Do this on both sides of one petal. Remove the freezer paper from the petal you just cut.

Cut along the inside perforated edge of the dart.

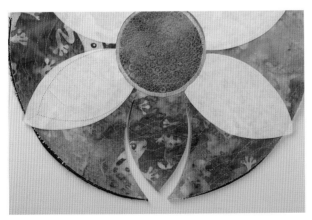

Darts for one petal cut

5. Use a zigzag stitch to sew one side of the petal, gently pulling the edges together. The edge of the

sandwich will stick out farther than the end of the petal. Leave it for now.

6. Zigzag up the second side of the petal. Stop about an inch before you get to the top of the petal.

7. Overlap the points and trim them even. Then trim just a tiny bit more off one side so the bowl will continue to round up.

Overlap the points and trim them.

8. Finish sewing the dart.

One petal with darts stitched

easy!

Apply fusible web to a "background" fabric. Cut the darts for 2 adjoining petals, and fuse a piece of the fabric to the fabric between the petals. Trim it to shape before sewing the darts. Be sure the fused background fabric goes clear to the base, and restitch around the base after shaping the bowl if desired. (See variations D and E, page 29.)

9. Trim the thread ends at the base after stitching each petal so they don't get caught in the next dart.

10. Repeat this process until you have cut and stitched a dart on each side of each petal.

All the darts are sewn.

11. Make any shape adjustments you want, and then sew over each dart line with a satin stitch.

fun!

Vary the number and size of petals for an entirely different flower!

fast!

Try this one with fast2fuse. Eliminate the surface quilting, and add an extra layer of fast2fuse under the fabric of the base on one side of the sandwich. Fuse the fabric to the fast2fuse, and then use steam and press firmly to adhere the extra base piece.

Finishing

1. Trim the edge so no canvas shows. Be sure to check from both sides.

2. Add the cording (page 9) as you satin stitch around the outer edge. Add a second layer of satin stitching if desired.

3. Embellish as you wish!

Sunflower bowl in different colors

Now you're ready to send some sunshine to your friends and family!

Variations

Fun in the sun—make your own bouquet of sunflowers for the summer or winter. By changing the colors and petal shapes, you can change the mood of this bowl and still keep it cheery and uplifting.

A. Trim the background, shape it a bit, fuse another color over it, and you have a flower with double the petals.

B. Round the petals and the background for a soft summer flower.

C. Change the look entirely by making the petals smaller and the background into leaves.

D. Choose a striking background and embellish the petals for a very modern flower.

E. Freehand cut the sandwich, cut the background out, and flip it over when making the petals for a casual-looking sunflower.

F. Petals, petals, and more petals! If six are not enough, just add more.

A

Blue, 2-color bowl, by Sidnee Snell

B

Round petal edges, by Libby Ankarberg

C

Ginkgo Bowl, by Kim Campbell

D

Modern flower bowl, by Marc Kemper

F

Multipetal bowl, by Kim Campbell

E

Fern background, Sunflower Bowl, by Linda Johansen

fluted bowl

Very graceful and flowing, but still formal, a Fluted Bowl can decorate your table all by itself. Add a candle or vase of flowers in it, and you have a lovely centerpiece. The shape works beautifully with floral fabrics.

What You'll Need

- ☐ 2 fat quarters of fabric
- ☐ ½ yard of unwashed heavyweight canvas, denim, or duck fabric
- ☐ 1 yard of fusible web
- ☐ 1½ yards of cording
- ☐ Temporary adhesive basting spray
- ☐ Topstitch needle (80/12 or 90/16)

- ☐ Template material for dart shapes (optional)
- ☐ Basic supplies (pages 8–9)

fun!

Change the size of the sandwich you start with, change the size or shape of the base, change the dart shapes—it's your bowl!

How-Tos

Layering

1. Cut 2 layers each of fabric, canvas, and fusible web to a circle approximately 16˝ in diameter. See page 10 for circle making methods.

fast!

Fuse the fabric to the canvas pieces first, then cut out two large circles.

2. Iron a piece of fusible web to the back of each circle of fabric and then fuse a fabric circle to each canvas circle.

Adding the Bases

1. Cut two 4˝ canvas circles for the base (page 10).

2. Lightly spray temporary adhesive on the canvas side of one layer of your sandwich.

3. Center one 4˝ canvas base on the sticky canvas. Before you spray, you can carefully measure to center or just eyeball it.

4. Lightly spray this 4˝ circle, and put the second one on top of it.

5. Lay the other 16˝ circle on top, canvas side down, fabric side up. If it doesn't hold, turn it over and *lightly* spray the canvas side. Press the canvas sides together firmly with your hands.

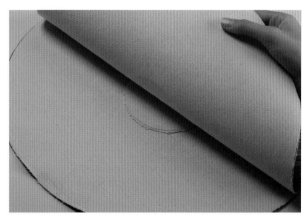

Center the two bases inside the canvas layers.

Quilting

Your quilting of the whole sandwich is enough if you don't want the stitching as a design element accentuating the base.

1. Mark an indentation at the edge of the base on one side by firmly pressing around it with your fingernail or a blunt point, such as a pen with the ink cartridge retracted. (Be sure to clean the point of the pen before using it.) Use a quilt marking pencil or chalk if you can't see the indentations.

Mark around the base with a blunt point.

2. Sew around the circle on this indented mark with a straight stitch to mark the base clearly.

3. Cover the straight stitch with a 4.0–width satin stitch. Anchor your stitches with a few short-length straight stitches at the end, right beside the satin stitch.

easy!

Lower the pressure on your presser foot for sewing on the base, if your machine has that option.

4. Sew within the base to anchor the layers together.

fun!

Sew the entire surface with the same stitches—stippling or following the fabric pattern without accenting the base.

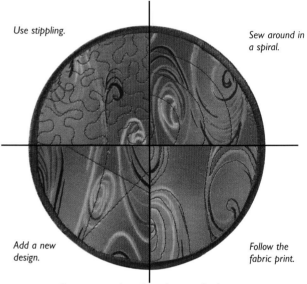

Use stippling.

Sew around in a spiral.

Add a new design.

Follow the fabric print.

Some examples of stitching in the base.

5. Shorten your straight stitch (2.0 length). Begin stitching to the right of the base. Anchor your stitching with a few short stitches just outside the satin stitching. Turn the sandwich counterclockwise while sewing so that the amount of fabric under the arm of your machine becomes less as you sew. (See step 1, page 25.)

6. Stitch the sides with an ever-widening wavy spiral or stippling, or just follow lines in the fabric. To make waves, hold the left edge with your hand and gently guide the edge back and forth as you sew around. Cross lines randomly as you sew. The surface works best with lots of stitching to hold the layers together when you cut darts.

Make your stippling loopy so you don't have to worry about crossing lines: Do it once, it's a mistake. Do it twice, it's a pattern!

fast!

Do all the stitching without stopping. Sew within the base, straight stitch around it, cover the straight stitch with satin stitching, then shorten your stitch length, and move right on to the wavy spiral stitching.

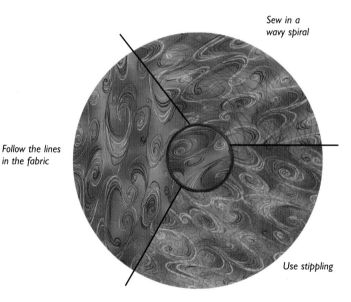

Sew in a wavy spiral

Follow the lines in the fabric

Use stippling

Three stitching options

Shaping

1. Mark the placement of 5 darts by inserting 5 pins spaced fairly evenly around the base of your sandwich.

Insert pins evenly spaced for 5 darts.

fun!

Darts *don't* have to be evenly spread around the bowl.

2. Using a marker, trace 5 darts using the pattern on page 45. Place the dart point $\frac{1}{8}$″–$\frac{1}{4}$″ from the edge of the base satin stitching.

Mark the darts.

fun!

Vary the shape on a couple of the darts to add variety to your bowl.

3. Cut the first dart on the marked lines and remove the dart's center.

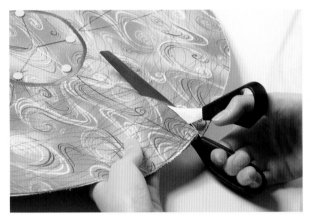

Cut the first dart.

4. Set your machine for a wide (4.5 or 5) zigzag stitch. Test your stitching on scraps of the canvas and fabric.

5. Begin sewing near the edge of the base, just before the dart begins. Gently and *firmly* pull the edges together to meet just ahead of the needle. It does take some muscle because the edges come up steeply at first.

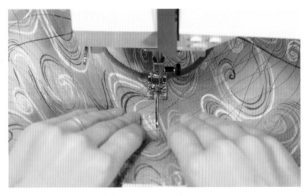

Firmly pull the edges together as you sew.

6. As you sew the dart, pull outward so that the dart edges just meet. The excess fabric is what causes the edge to ripple so nicely!

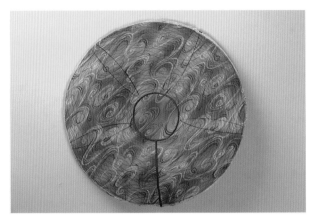

One dart sewn

7. Trim the thread ends at the base after each line of stitching so they don't get caught in the next darts.

8. Repeat this process until you have cut and stitched each dart.

9. Go over each dart with a satin stitch. Remember to backstitch a few stitches to the edge of the base when you begin sewing up the dart. This will lock your stitches.

Finishing

1. Trim the outer edge of the bowl.

2. Zigzag the cording on (page 9), then satin stitch around the outer edge. For a smoother finished look, add a second layer of satin stitching.

Another version of the fluted bowl

Love those fly away edges!

Variations

Try changing the shape of the sandwich, the shape of the darts, or even adding a center for some interesting and exciting variations. Add a contrasting center to carry through on a theme.

A. Try on the darts out a geometric bowl with some Timtex or fast2fuse.

B. Canvas can go square, too!

C. This sweet little bowl has the widest part of the dart close to the center.

D. Hearts and tiny stippling send a heartfelt message to a friend.

E. The free-form shape and ribbon edging add whimsy to this fluted heart bowl.

F. You can change the shape of the darts, still butting them together, and then appliqué stones and add decorative stitching, I did for this commissioned piece.

Square bowl from *Fast, Fun & Easy Fabric Bowls*, with fluted darts, by Linda Johansen

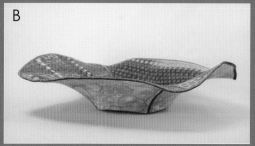

Square fluted bowl, by Alex Vincent

Different-shaped dart in small, hand-dyed "plate", by Linda Johansen

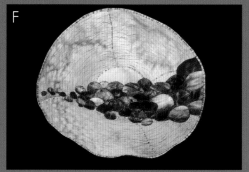

Bowl with appliquéd stones and decorative stitching, by Linda Johansen, courtesy of Loreen Olufson

Bowl of hearts and tiny stippling, by Linda Johansen

Fluted Heart Bowl, by Kim Campbell

fantasy flower bowl

Make your fantasy garden come true with a big bouquet of these bowls—fun in any size or shape.

What You'll Need

- ☐ 2 fat quarters of solid or nearly solid fabric, so that the decorative stitching will show
- ☐ 2 scraps, approximately 5″ square, of fabric for flower center
- ☐ ½ yard of canvas, denim, or duck fabric
- ☐ 1 yard of fusible web
- ☐ 4–6 colors of thread to coordinate or contrast with flower fabrics
- ☐ 3 yards of cording
- ☐ Temporary adhesive basting spray
- ☐ Topstitch needle (90/14)
- ☐ Pattern for petals (page 45)
- ☐ Basic supplies (pages 8–9)

Note: Be sure your machine can stitch through 4 layers of your chosen stabilizer plus 2 layers of fabrics.

How-Tos

Layering

1. Iron fusible web to the wrong side of two 15″ squares of fabric. Peel off the paper backing from the fabric squares, and fuse them to two 15″ squares of canvas.

2. Draw a 14″ circle on the fabric side of one fused pieced and cut it out using scissors or a rotary cutter. See page 10 for circle making methods.

Use a plate and freehand cut your circle. Flowers aren't perfectly round, especially fantasy flowers!

3. Lightly spray the canvas side of half of the sandwich with temporary spray adhesive. On a flat surface, firmly press the canvas sides together to hold the sandwich layers until you sew them.

4. Stack the layers, and place the stack on a cutting mat. Use a large rotary cutter, and press firmly to cut through all the layers on the marked circle.

Use a plate to hold the layers and to keep your fingers out of the way of the rotary cutter.

Adding the Bases

1. Iron fusible web to the wrong side of two 5″ scraps of flower center fabric and to one side of two 5″ scraps of canvas.

2. Use a compass to draw a 3½″ circle on the paper backing of the fusible web on one of the canvas pieces (page 10). Cut on the marked circle. *Do not mark or cut the other canvas scrap.*

Fussy cut a center, or dye or paint your own.

fast!

3. Cut only one fabric base ¹⁄₁₆″ larger all around than the canvas circle. Do this by adding ⅛″ to the circle size of your compass, or pin the pieces together and cut the fabric larger. *Do not cut the second fabric scrap.*

Cut the fabric base ¹⁄₁₆″ larger all around than the canvas base.

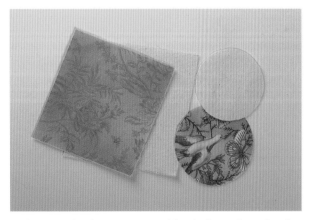

These are the 4 pieces you need for the base of your bowl.

4. Take the paper backing off, and place the canvas circle in the center of the sandwich—eyeball it; it's a flower! Fuse the canvas base to the sandwich.

Canvas base fused to center of sandwich

easy!

5. With temporary basting spray, *very lightly* spray the second, untrimmed canvas base and stick it on the other side of the fabric sandwich. Check carefully to be sure that it is centered over the first base.

6. Slightly shorten your stitch length to 2.0. Use any color thread, and with the untrimmed base on the bottom, straight stitch around the first, cutout canvas base. Keep your stitching ¹⁄₁₆″ to the inside of the edge.

Stitch 1/16″ inside the edge of the canvas.

7. Turn the sandwich over, and pull up on the canvas while you trim away the excess beyond the stitching. Your bases will line up perfectly using this method.

8. Iron the canvas you just trimmed to fuse it in place.

easy!

Use your double-curved appliqué scissors, and pull up firmly on the fabric to get as close as possible to the stitching for a nice, clean edge.

9. Repeat the same steps for fusing, sewing, and trimming the fabric bases. Be sure to line up the first fabric with the canvas, and check carefully that it is centered.

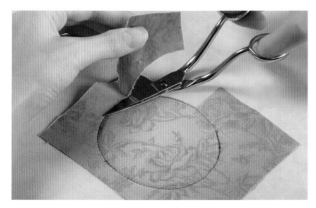

Trim the fabric close to the stitching so the edges on both sides match.

Quilting the Base

1. Sew some "flower-like" stitching in the base to stabilize it. An easy way to do "free-motion look-alike" is to shorten the stitch length to 2.0 and straight stitch around a motif in the base fabric.

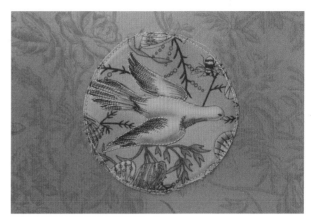

Follow a fabric motif for stabilizing the base.

2. A more decorative stitch, such as an open star or asterisk-like stitch, gives a fun look, too. This is also a good place to try some free-motion quilting—especially if you have fussy cut a center to follow the lines. See page 10 for more instructions on free-motion quilting.

Check your machine for other fun stitches for stabilizing the base.

fun!

Do random stitching on the canvas base before adding the fabric bases. When you fuse on the fabrics, they will hide your stitching, and show off the base fabric more. This works especially well if you have fussy cut a motif from your fabric and don't want to do free-motion quilting.

3. Set your machine for a tight (.2), medium-width (4.0) satin stitch. Practice your stitches on a scrap that is the same thickness as your sandwich.

4. Satin-stitch around the edge of the base. Be aware that your machine is sewing with 4 layers of canvas and 4 layers each of fabric and fusible on one side of the needle and 2 layers of each on the other side. You will need to gently help guide the sandwich, as the feed dogs won't be helping much on the side with less fabric thickness.

5. End the stitching with a few very fine straight stitches along the edge of the satin stitching.

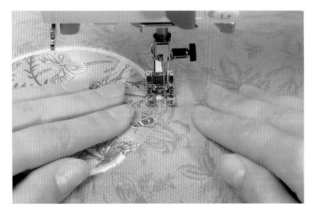

Gently help guide the sandwich.

easy!

If your satin stitches don't quite cover the edge of the base on the bottom side, just flip the sandwich over and sew around again with a wider satin stitch.

Quilting the Petals

1. Copy the pattern on page 45 for the petals. Draw 5 petals on the sandwich with a marking pencil or pen that you can see easily. Everyone's center and sandwich will be slightly different—just trim or shift the template a bit to fit the petals on.

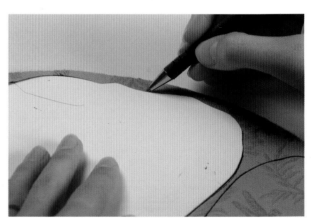

Draw 5 petals on the sandwich.

fun!

This is a great project to try colorful threads.

2. Straight stitch around the drawn petals with thread that is easy to see. This stabilizes the sandwich while you are quilting the petals.

3. Thread the machine with a decorative thread, drop or cover the feed dogs on your machine, and put on a darning foot.

4. Loosen the top tension to about 2.5 and place the needle at the inside edge of a petal. Sew while pulling the sandwich toward and away from yourself as you turn it.

Note: Remember to practice first on scrap or between the petals. See page 10 for more instructions on free-motion quilting.

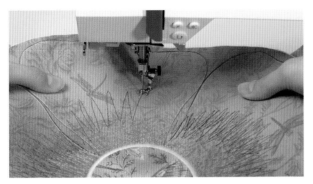

Pull the sandwich toward and away from yourself to get spiky points.

easy!

Not comfortable with free-motion stitching? Set your machine for a straight stitch. Sew in a straight line out toward the edge and back toward the center, forming spiky lines. Do this by sewing out with your machine set on backstitch, and then sewing forward toward the center. Random is good here!

5. Sew spikes around the base with one color thread, with the spikes going about 2″ out from the center.

6. Change your thread to the next color and repeat the spiky stitching out another 2″–3″. Repeat with each color of thread, overlapping colors a bit for a nice blend.

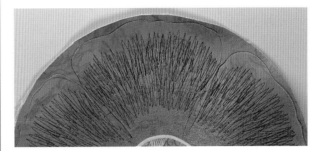

Overlap the colors a bit to blend them.

fun!

Use variegated threads and keep the colors together: Sew closer to the base when the thread is light, and farther out when the thread is dark.

7. Add some accent threads for pizzazz—maybe another color or a different texture.

A Fantasy Flower Bowl in the making with the accent stitching completed

Finishing the Petals

1. Stitch again around the petal edges with a shortened straight stitch (1.5 or so). This anchors any stitches that go over the line you will cut.

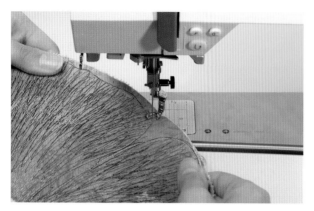

Stitch around the petal edges to hold the free-motion quilting threads.

2. Trim around the petals, with scissors, just outside the sewn lines.

3. Begin zigzagging the cording onto the side of this first petal (page 9). Anchor it on with a few stitches in place.

Trim the petals and apply cording around each petal.

4. Continue applying the cording around each petal. Leave the needle down on the outside of the cording when you turn the corner at the base to make sure it stays in the corner.

fast!

You can satin stitch around each petal after it is cut without putting cording on. It's your flower!

5. Satin stitch around the edge of each petal. If needed, satin stitch each one a second time.

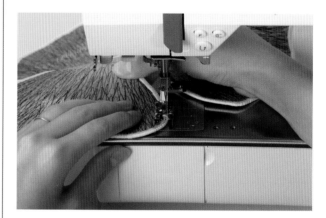

Satin stitch over the cording.

fun!

Start with a narrower stitch at the base of the petal and graduate to a wider stitch along the outer edge.

Shaping

1. Pull the petals so that each overlaps the one next to it, and pin them in place. Play with it until you get the shape you like.

Use sturdy pins to hold the petals.

2. When you like the shape, thread your machine with the color of thread you used for the quilting where the petals will overlap, and add a few more spiky lines to hold the petals together. Begin and end with lockstitches each time.

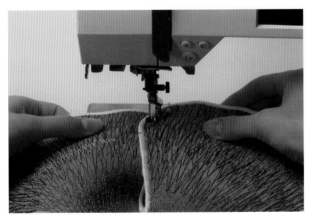

Use a matching thread to sew the overlapped petals.

easy!

Leave the pin in to hold the shape when you start stitching. Remember to pull it out before you sew over it!

fun!

Stitch the petals together closer to the base, and let the petals flare out a bit.

Different finished fantasy bowl, by Linda Johansen

Now you're ready to create a whole garden!

Variations

A little fantasy never hurt anyone...make yours floral!

A. These petals were cut gently curving and lower on one corner.

B. Kim actually made one and a half bowls, doubling the base for this realistic pansy.

C. The dogwoods were blooming when this bowl came to life.

D. Shape four petals differently and a California poppy pops out!

E. It doesn't have to be a flower. Japanese fabrics, gentle curves, and overlapped shapes create a bowl with simple elegance.

F. Another sweet one! Gently rounded petals, contrasting thread, and fun quilting combine for this garden flower.

Hand-dyed Pinwheel Bowl, by Linda Johansen

Pansy Bowl, by Kim Campbell

Dogwood Bowl, by Sidnee Snell

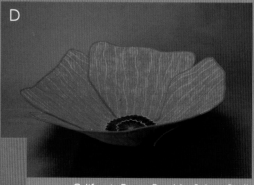
California Poppy Bowl, by Sidnee Snell

Floral Print Bowl,
by Kim Campbell

Simple Japanese bowl, by Linda Johansen

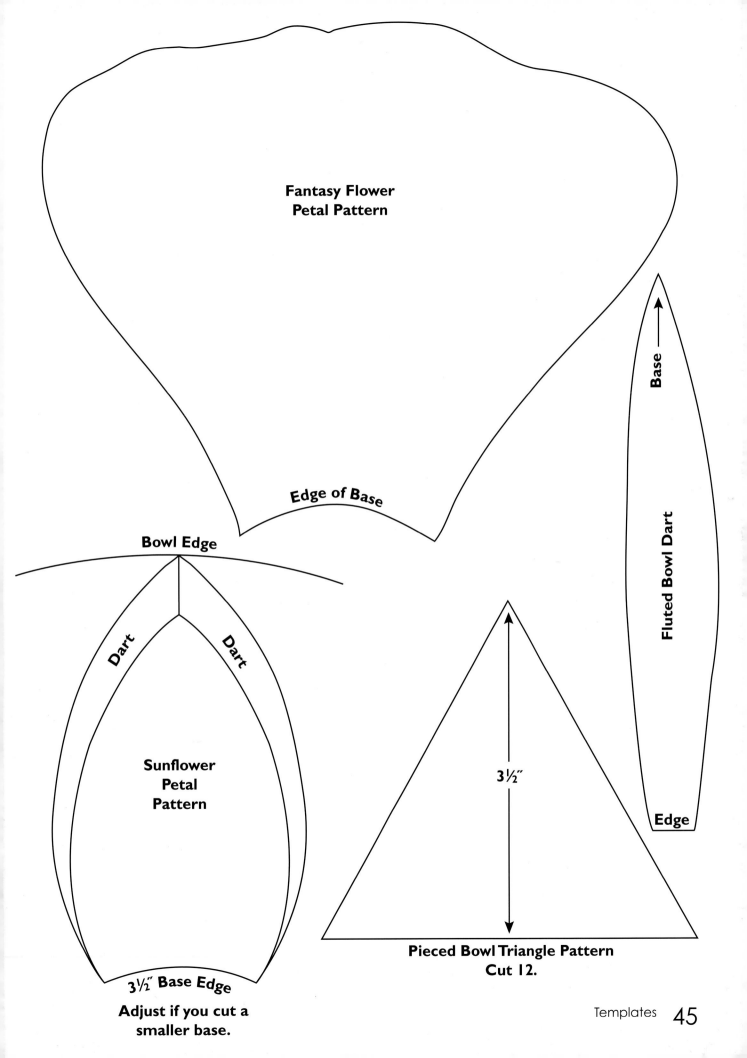

**Fantasy Flower
Petal Pattern**

Base

Edge of Base

Fluted Bowl Dart

Bowl Edge

Dart   **Dart**

**Sunflower
Petal
Pattern**

3½″

Edge

**Pieced Bowl Triangle Pattern
Cut 12.**

3½″ **Base Edge**

**Adjust if you cut a
smaller base.**

embellishments

Adding your own touches to the bowls is probably the most fun part of making them. Little additions or changes can make them uniquely yours—for you or friends and family to treasure. Take an excursion to look around the house or craft store for treasures that would make your bowls say, "This is *me*!"

Ribbon-edged Heart Bowl, by Kim Campbell

Accent thread and center stitching add texture to Ginkgo Bowl, by Kim Campbell

A. Ribbon Folded ribbons add a true "from the heart" message to this bowl.

B. Threads Sparkly thread and lots of surface stitching can add great texture.

C. Yarn Couching yarn—zigzagging over it with an invisible thread or one that blends—on the edge will change the impact of the bowl. Plus Kim will do anything to get out of satin stitching!

D. Quilting Decorative free-motion quilting can also change the character of your bowl. I really like lots of thread decorating a bowl—can you tell?

E. Fusing Fusing shapes and fun stitching can take the bowl from fun to art.

F. Fabric Using the fabric motif for a quilting pattern can create a simple elegance. It also can make decisions easier.

Couched yarn edge on Pansy Bowl, by Kim Campbell

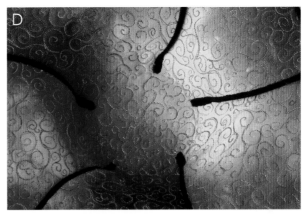

Swirly quilting, by Linda Johansen

Fluted Stones Bowl, by Linda Johansen,
courtesy of Loreen Olufson

Fluted Bowl with quilting around leaves, by Linda Johansen

Couched yarn and beads on Lilac Bowl, by Kim Campbell

Crazy Quilt Bowl, by Linda Johansen

G. Beads Couching yarn and adding beads created a fun floral theme on this large Lilac Bowl.

H. Scraps and Stitches I had such a good time with this bowl—trying out all the great stitches on my machine, choosing all the threads, and using up scraps that already had fusible on them from other bowls!

About the Author

by John Halley

Linda Johansen lives with her husband in the lush Willamette Valley, in Corvallis, Oregon. Now that their sons are grown up, they are enjoying adjusting to living without children. First on the agenda was a studio expansion for Linda for all the bowls and boxes that were flowing into the living room—and they still left rooms for both boys to come visit.

Linda enjoys creating fun new projects for others to enjoy, gardening, bird-watching, cycling, dyeing her own fabrics, dancing with her husband, and the company of old faithful dogs. She has had a lot less time for all but the last two since the publication of *Fast, Fun & Easy Fabric Bowls* and *Fast, Fun & Easy Fabric Boxes*. And now *Fast, Fun & Easy Irresist-A-Bowls*!

The author can be reached at info@lindajohansen.com. And be sure to check out her website, www.lindajohansen.com, to see where she will be teaching next.

Resources

All of the materials and tools mentioned in this book should be available at your local quilt shop or one of the companies listed below.

fast2fuse

C&T Publishing

1-800-284-1114

www.ctpub.com

Timtex

Timber Lane Press

1-800-752-3353 (wholesale only)

email: qltblox@earthlink.net

General quilting supplies and products mentioned in this book are available by mail order from these companies:

A Common Thread

16925 SW 65th

Lake Oswego, OR 97035

1-877-915-6789 (toll free)

email: actbernina@aol.com

www.acommonthreadfabrics.com

Cotton Patch Mail Order

3405 Hall Lane, Dept. CTB

Lafayette, CA 94549

1-800-835-4418

email: quiltusa@yahoo.com

www.quiltusa.com